Library of Congress Control Number:
2020911696

ISBN 978-0-9824723-6-1

Copyright 2021, by Be Be

All rights reserved
Published in the United States of America
By High Touch LLC

Published February 14, 2021

To submit reviews please visit
www.GreatUrantianAgreement.com

Urantia Book quotation legend
paper#: section#, paragraph#
i.e., 93: 4. 3 and 55: 3. 2

Cover illustration by Be Be

Table of Contents

Preface 3

When You Wish Upon a Star 5

The URANTIA Book: The 5th Epochal Revelation to the People of Planet Earth 7

Now for Some History According to the Urantia Book 27

Paper 91 The Evolution of Prayer 33

Believe 63

Dreaming is a Skill of Believing/Thinking/Imagining 71

God Promises 77

Following God's Instructions 85

We Must Focus on God's Promises 99

Samples of God's Promises! 105

God Will Take Care of Everything! 115

Bliss 121

Afterword 129

Acknowledgements

*I have tremendous gratitude in my heart for the support and encouragement from so many; some of whom I hereby recognize:
Marie, Cathy, Steven, David, Kenneth, Jim, Mike, William, Julz, Anji, Moses, Elizabeth, Michael, Jill, Pete, Jeanette, Sharon, Bobbie, JoAnn, Paula, Moe, Tim, Melissa, Mary Jo, Dave, Adrienne, Capt. Flashback, Jolene, Jesus and The Angel with No Name, and special thanks to my brilliant sister Carrie whose editing skills made this book spectacular.*

Thank you all!

Preface

There may be times when those around us call out the old saying: "If wishes were horses, then beggars would ride." I was taught this to be a quote of derision toward wish making or an attempt at discouraging the effort of making wishes. I'm sure if those recalling this quote would look beneath the surface, they would find a marvelous array of processes that support proper wish making.

When young, we may have been bullied for our dreaming, by older siblings or classmates, and so we learned to Poo Poo our own dreams and give up without even trying. In order to overcome this tendency, we must recognize the "mental tour guides" for guilt trips that we unknowingly created. We must replace them with tour guides that can showcase positive vistas filled with truth, beauty, and goodness.

I wrote this treatise because I felt I found something of value. Not just for some, but for everyone. And now I am showcasing this fabulous agreement because it is...
FABULOUS!

I'm making such a big 'to do' about wishes because "Wishing" introduces the topic of this book. Wishing, or willing goodness to come into our lives is an innate tendency built into our minds by our creator. Desiring things helps us make sense of our world as a place where we can grow both materially and spiritually.

Our creator gave us free will and a way to use that free will. Understanding the proper use of free will helps us as we mature into healthy participants in this realm of heaven on earth.

God doesn't have any grandchildren. We are all directly related and designed to enjoy a world that is both nurturing and growth stimulating. The child of a cat grows up to be a cat. The child of a dog grows up to be a dog. We, the children of God, must sooner or later grow up. This book is designed to foster a sense of growing up.

When You Wish Upon A Star

"I've only got dimes and nickels for change. I'm sorry," said the cashier. "That's alright," I exclaimed, "I do appreciate your service, and your smile." Her face lit up and as I left the store, I felt the weight of the silver coins in my palm. "Hmm, I wonder," I thought out loud to myself, "if I place these coins here on the sidewalk, will anyone notice them and pick them up?"

Upon reaching my truck I could see the shiny pile gleaming back at me. Waiting and watching, 30 minutes seemed like hours. All sorts of people, young and old passed by. The little pile of gleaming money continued sitting there. I thought about how many times in my past I also passed by wealth or an opportunity that was just sitting out in the open, waiting for someone to notice. I mused over how excited I would get after finding someone's lost change as a child. I remembered how lucky it always felt to find that $20.00 bill I forgot in my jacket pocket.

Daydreams like this, focus my quest to keep a lookout for hidden treasures in ordinary places.

The URANTIA Book:
The 5th Epochal Revelation to the People of Planet Earth

All around us are clues for success. We need only to open our mind to see the possibilities for solutions to the many problems that beset us daily. Sometimes, magnificent resources are introduced to us through friends. This happened to me in 1978 when my friend Pete showed me a very large book and told me to "just scan the table of contents."

I couldn't believe the topics listed. I remember thinking, "Wow! Are all these things actually addressed in this book?"

Turns out the book he showed me, The Urantia Book, was not just a book, but a revelation to our world about how things got to be the way they are today. So, the next day I went to the bookstore and bought myself a copy.

The Urantia Book began to feed my hunger for more information about the history of our world and our local universe as revealed by those with seemingly first-hand knowledge of its unfolding.

The book I would find, addressed information regarding creation, by the way of evolution, of our planet Earth, and how our world, aka Urantia, fits into the universe at large.

The Urantia Book represents the 5th Epochal revelation to the people of Planet Earth. The topic of my book however, refers to the 3rd Epochal revelation; the arrival of Melchizedek. Melchizedek was a very important religious teacher, who appeared 4,000 years ago on an emergency mission to Earth to keep alive the awareness of there being only one God.

For more information regarding an overview of this wondrous book please visit the following website: *truthbook.com/*

To my delight, after a bit of studying, The Urantia Book turned out to make a great deal of sense.

I found the intelligence illuminating. The information revealed in the book retained the same sense of sanity regarding science, religion, and philosophy from the beginning to its end. It took me about one year to finish my first reading. Mind you, this book is two inches thick with 2097 onion thin pages.

One of my favorite memories happened in 1979 as I was sitting on the top of Berthoud Pass in Colorado. After riding the gondola to the peak to enjoy the view and have lunch, it was with a sense of reverence; I read the last two chapters.

Afterwards, mesmerized by the beauty of the surrounding mountain tops, I thought to myself, "Wow! Did this book really say what I think it said? I must read again and pay closer attention." So off I went and read it another time… many times. So far I've read the book from cover to cover, page by page, and word for word, 9 times.

During my seventh time through the book, I noticed something that stood out like a very colorful rainbow following an afternoon rain shower. It mentions a 4,000-year-old agreement between God and Man; between Divinity and Humanity.

When I read the following quote from the book, I thought about it for quite some time.

> *"This covenant of Melchizedek with Abraham represents the great Urantian agreement between divinity and humanity whereby God agrees to do 'every-thing'; man only agrees to 'believe' God's promises and follow his instructions."* The Urantia Book 93:6.4

There was something to this quote, which moved me to do something to make it more widely known. Perhaps the Angels of Marketing were inspiring me to re-package this part of the revelation from The Urantia Book and showcase this Great Urantian Agreement by putting it on the shelf for everyone to read.

Maybe then, they would be inspired to find a copy of The Urantia Book and read it for themselves. And maybe, it would inspire people to become the promise-making dreamers we were originally designed to be. We are star-making *wishing machines,* and as we blossom in our maturity, heaven transforms earth.

Four thousand years ago, a wondrous statement, this Great Urantian Agreement, echoed throughout the lands and then became forgotten in time. I've concluded that quote has been kept secret for some reason. I'm amazed no one seems to recall anything about it. It isn't mentioned in any of the fairy tales I've heard of, or found in legends passed down like old wives' tales. "If this is so great," I wondered, "then why don't more people know about it? Why don't they talk about this in church?"

I understand the Great Agreement to contain three main parts. First, there is the statement that God will take care of everything. Second, there is the statement that all we have to do is believe in promises and third, that we follow directions once they are given to us.

1. God takes care of everything
2. We believe in Gods promises
3. Follow the instructions, His directions.

Little did I know the theme of this Great Agreement came to life in 1940 in a secular song written by Leigh Harline and Ned Washington, and showcased in Disney's movie, Pinocchio, sung by the animated Jiminy Cricket.

At this point, I would like to direct you online to find the lyrics of the song, "When You Wish Upon A Star." Please read the lyrics of the entire song, or listen to it to understand how attractive it would be to declare your wishes.

I would have included the lyrics to the song here, but when I asked the copyright owner for reprint permission, I was denied. No matter, it's a great song and has a great message. Please go listen to it.

In this case, the Star represents Divinity and although simple, this Great Urantian Agreement between Deity and Humanity has resurfaced as one of the most powerful and result producing concepts available to us. We have great untapped potential within us as dream makers. Our ultimate job and pastime is to dream. To be a dream wisher! A dream fulfiller!

If you could suspend judgment and agree at this point, to recognize God as the Star we wish upon, then everything about this Great Agreement would fall into place and make great sense to you. So, while reading the rest of this book please do yourself a favor and understand that when we speak of God, we are referring to this lovely Divine celestial being called "Star".

By the way, I don't mean for this book to come across like religious propaganda. Many will see it as such, but please don't let this deter you from understanding that this Great Urantian Agreement is available to you in this life.

Fundamental world religions, mainly Jewish, Christian and Islamic dogmas currently understand the Great Urantian Agreement to be regarded as the "Abrahamic Covenant." I speculate this is so because this part of the "covenant" happened concurrently, 4,000 years ago.

The "Abrahamic Covenant" contains three main features defined as follows;

1. The promise of land Genesis 12:1.
2. The promise of descendants Genesis 12:2.
3. The promise of blessings and redemption Genesis 12:3.

Over time, the Judeo-Christian, Islamic version of the Abrahamic covenant has been morphed by men into promoting a "Chosen People" idea;

an idea that some people are chosen over others because they "believe" in a certain way. What is not understood, and remains unspoken when believing this "Chosen People" theory is the ideal that all people are chosen. God loves all the children not just the children of certain believers of a certain religion. Not naming any names.

"For I am persuaded, that neither death, nor life, nor angels, nor principalities, nor powers, nor things present, nor things to come, nor height, nor depth, nor any other creature, shall be able to separate us from the love of God."
Romans 8:38-39

The Great Urantian Agreement, quoted from the Urantia Book is the premium topic for this dissertation. This Treatise will delve deeply into The Great Urantian Agreement between Divinity and Humanity stated again as follows: *"This covenant of Melchizedek with Abraham represents the great Urantian agreement between divinity and humanity whereby God agrees to do 'every-thing'; man only agrees to 'believe' God's promises and follow his instructions."* The Urantia Book 93:6.4

WOW! That alone is incredible enough as it seems. This quotation contains some very interesting possibilities. Let me state it again. "God agrees to do *everything*; man (& woman) only agrees to *believe* God's promises and follow God's instructions." God agrees to keep the sun shining and the moon circling the earth, and the flowers budding and fruit trees blooming and fish swimming. God agrees to take care of the beating hearts in each one of us, and to take us home to a better place when it's time for us to die. God agrees to take care of "everything." We simply agree to "believe" in God's promises and "follow" His instructions.

This is a conditional and bilateral agreement in which each of the parties involved, apply themselves to the fulfillment of their part of the bargain whether the other party is fulfilling theirs, or not.

This is the true meaning of "Giving without thought of return;" the purest form of good will toward others.

I find that the most useful time to employ the effects of following the Great Agreements' Directives is when I worry. At the time of becoming depressed through worry, I find myself speaking with Star and praying for a solution, or assistance from His angels. Then, I remember this agreement and apply my acceptance of it. I ask God for directions to an answer, a solution, a response of health or guidance. I find myself formulating requests for promises to be made and directions to be inspired.

Said Jesus to his followers: *"Ask and it shall be given you; seek, and you shall find; knock, and the door shall be opened unto you."* Matthew 7:7

All prayers or requests for promises, need not be self-less; we do need to learn to speak up for ourselves as well for as others. I no longer see my prayers as being only for spiritual things or solely material things. I recognize that Star will see fit to bring me what-so-ever I need to grow and learn from experiencing life. I relax my anxieties and remove the stress of so many distractions. I listen for instructions from Star and continue to believe in the promises I've asked Star for; the wishes I've made upon the Star.

In The Urantia Book; it's revealed, *"On a mortal-bestowal mission a Paradise Son is always born of woman and grows up as a male child of the realm, as Jesus did on Urantia. These Sons of supreme service all pass from infancy through youth to manhood just as does a human being. In every respect they become like the mortals of the race into which they are born.* **They make petitions to the Father** *as do the children of the realms in which they serve."* The Urantia Book: 20:6.2

This being the case, I am going to follow the lead of these Paradise Sons and learn how to "petition" the Father/Mother God/Star in this realm where I live and breathe. By the way, it also says, *"All genuine spirit-born petitions are certain of an answer. Ask and you shall receive."* The Urantia Book: 168:4.12

Learn how to pray. Learn how to wish. I came to this realization when I found myself staring blankly into the darkness before sleep. I needed to learn how to petition God for promises; to learn how to creatively allow God to help make my prayers and dreams come true. I thought to myself, "Perhaps make my wishes known to God by first asking; How?"

What are the techniques for believing? What is the substance of believing? How do I ask for what I want? What kinds of things should I ask for? What kinds of things can I ask for? Is there a menu of selections available? How can I too, petition the Father? How can I think my thoughts and formulate ideas or imagine expressions that may evoke meaningful and worthwhile consequences? How do I pray?

2,000 years ago, Jesus' answers to his disciples many questions regarding prayer may be summarized as follows:

1. *Prayer is an expression of the finite mind in an effort to approach the Infinite. The making of a prayer must, therefore, be limited by the knowledge, wisdom, and attributes of the finite; likewise must the answer be conditioned by the vision, aims, ideals, and prerogatives of the Infinite. There never can be observed an unbroken continuity of material phenomena between the making of a prayer and the reception of the full spiritual answer thereto.*
The Urantia Book: 168:4.3

2. *When a prayer is apparently unanswered, the delay often betokens a better answer, although one which is for some good reason greatly* delayed. When Jesus said that Lazarus's sickness was really not to the death, he had already been dead eleven hours. No sincere prayer is denied an answer except when the superior viewpoint of the spiritual world has devised a better answer, an answer which meets the petition of the spirit of man as contrasted with the prayer of the mere mind of man. The Urantia Book: 168:4.4

3. The prayers of time, when indited by the spirit and expressed in faith, are often so vast and all-encompassing that they can be answered only in eternity; the finite petition is sometimes so fraught with the grasp of the Infinite that the answer must long be postponed to await the creation of adequate capacity for receptivity; the prayer of faith may be so all-embracing that the answer can be received only on Paradise. The Urantia Book: 168:4.5

4. The answers to the prayer of the mortal mind are often of such a nature that they can be received and recognized only after that same praying mind has attained the immortal state. The prayer of the material being can many times be answered only when such an individual has progressed to the spirit level. The Urantia Book: 168:4.6

5. *The prayer of a God-knowing person may be so distorted by ignorance and so deformed by superstition that the answer thereto would be highly undesirable. Then must the intervening spirit beings so translate such a prayer that, when the answer arrives, the petitioner wholly fails to recognize it as the answer to his prayer.* The Urantia Book: 168:4.7

6. *All true prayers are addressed to spiritual beings, and all such petitions must be answered in spiritual terms, and all such answers must consist in spiritual realities. Spirit beings cannot bestow material answers to the spirit petitions of even material beings. Material beings can pray effectively only when they "pray in the spirit."* The Urantia Book: 168:4.8

7. *No prayer can hope for an answer unless it is born of the spirit and nurtured by faith. Your sincere faith implies that you have in advance virtually granted your prayer hearers the full right to answer your petitions in accordance with that supreme wisdom and that divine love which your faith depicts as always actuating those beings to whom you pray.* The Urantia Book: 168:4.9

8. *The child is always within his rights when he presumes to petition the parent, and the parent is always within his parental obligations to the immature child when his superior wisdom dictates that the answer to the child's prayer be delayed, modified, segregated, transcended, or postponed to another stage of spiritual ascension.* The Urantia Book: 168:4.10

9. *Do not hesitate to pray the prayers of spirit longing; doubt not that you shall receive the answer to your petitions. These answers will be on deposit, awaiting your achievement of those future spiritual levels of actual cosmic attainment, on this world or on others, whereon it will become possible for you to recognize and appropriate the long-waiting answers to your earlier but ill-timed petitions.*
The Urantia Book: 168:4.11

10. *All genuine spirit-born petitions are certain of an answer. Ask and you shall receive. But you should remember that you are progressive creatures of time and space; therefore must you constantly reckon with the time-space factor in the experience of your personal reception of the full answers to your manifold prayers and petitions.* The Urantia Book: 168:4.12

A dear friend once wrote me saying, "I do believe that if we should dwell only on positive petitions for promises, this is what we will attract, yet trials of mistakes and shortcomings do come about. Maybe someone should write a treatise on blocking such trials and tribulations."

I personally choose to dwell only on positive, progressive approaches so I will never write such a treatise. I am reminded however that sometimes, prayers and petitions of promises seem to fall on deaf ears and go unfulfilled.

This is because this world was not meant to be a breeze for us; it wasn't meant to be a place where we get by on something for nothing. This life is for our growth as well as for stimulating our participation and enjoyment.

In a center for physical medicine and rehabilitation in New York City, a bronze plaque on the wall in the reception area displays the following poem, written by an unknown Civil War soldier.

The poem reads as follows:

"*I asked God for strength, that I might achieve.
I was made weak, that I might learn humbly to obey . . .*

*I asked for health, that I might do great things.
I was given infirmity that I might do better things . . .*

*I asked for riches, that I might be happy.
I was given poverty, that I might be wise . . .*

*I asked for power, that I might have the praise of men.
I was given weakness, that I might feel the praise of God . . .*

*I asked for things, that I might enjoy life.
I was given life, that I might enjoy things . . .*

*I got nothing I asked for—but everything I'd hoped for.
Almost despite myself, my unspoken prayers were answered.*

I am, among men, most richly blessed."

This soldier's faith, like that of Abraham, Isaac, Jacob, Mohammad and Jesus was awesome. Despite what life had promised and not delivered, our ancestors never lost their belief that life is filled with purpose and meaning. Somehow, they never gave up. They sustained an outlook that was built on faith and hope, and because of it, they nurtured better lives. That is the bottom line of our faith. Despite broken promises and disappointed expectations, we can live a powerful faith-filled life with meaning, purpose, and blessings.

There are many different types of things you can do with your prayer efforts. A very special form of prayer is called worship. You become what you worship. This function is where you place something on the altar of your attention and pay attention to it. This takes place when you appreciate stuff. That which you appreciate, multiplies. That which you appreciate becomes more so of whatever you are appreciating. The best thing to worship would of course be God's Creativity, God's Love, and God's presence. You are what you dwell upon in your mind. To think is to create. To praise is to appreciate. To adore is to become.

Yet we may find that deciding on where to live, what to wear, how to obtain money or find a career that may lead to a worthwhile standard of living, is more to our joy and liking. If so then, Great! So be it. Get ready! Things are about to change.

As I'm learning this concept for myself, I've been sharing the Great Agreement with my friends; encouraging them to check out the agreement for themselves. As a youth I was told, "If you wish to learn something, then go teach it."

Personally, achieving successful results encourages me to learn how to use the Great Agreement. It's in these moments I get to see God "taking care of everything," and I'm in awe with a lively sense of gratitude.

The Law of Attraction in effect states that you will attract what you are, not what you want or lack. Notice how a magnet will only attract more of what it is; steel. It will not attract gold, or something that it is not.

In the process of bringing our dreams to fruition, we need to discern the difference between the contrast of the wondrous aroma and beauty of the rose, verses the prick of the thorn. Subjective appreciation deepens our wealth of human understanding and broadens the meanings of values we share between us.

Now for Some History According to the Urantia Book

4,000 years ago, God revealed a code of behavior in which He laid out a list of instructions for us. The following describes how simple those instructions were.

On God's behalf, Melchizedek taught that salvation, survival beyond death, needed to be simply a matter of faith and trust in the one and only God. He taught so in a world where the norm was to have many gods; designer gods with various targets for prayers, gifts, and sacrifices; mainly through disciples, deacons, priests, popes, saints, prophets, and other "super heroes."

The Salem Religion

"The ceremonies of the Salem worship were very simple. Every person who signed or marked the clay-tablet rolls of the Melchizedek church committed to memory, and subscribed to, the following belief:

1. *I believe in El Elyon, the Most High God, the only Universal Father and Creator of all things.*

2. *I accept the Melchizedek covenant with the Most High, which bestows the favor of God on my faith, not on sacrifices and burnt offerings.*

3. *I promise to obey the seven commandments of Melchizedek and to **tell the good news of this covenant with the Most High to all men.**"*

And that was the whole of the creed of the Salem colony. But even such a short and simple declaration of faith was altogether too much and too advanced for the men of those days. They simply could not grasp the idea of getting divine favor for nothing – by faith. They were too deeply confirmed in the belief that man was born under forfeit to the gods. Too long and too earnestly had they sacrificed and made gifts to the priests to be able to comprehend the good news that salvation, divine favor, was a free gift to all who would believe in the Melchizedek covenant. But Abraham did believe halfheartedly, and even that was "counted for righteousness."

The seven commandments promulgated by Melchizedek were patterned along the lines of the ancient Dalamation supreme law, and very much resembled the seven commands taught in the first and second Gardens of Eden.

These commands of the Salem religion were:

1. *You shall not serve any God but the Most High Creator of heaven and earth.*

2. *You shall not doubt that faith is the only requirement for eternal salvation.*

3. *You shall not bear false witness (*or lie).*

4. *You shall not kill (*or murder).*

5. *You shall not steal.*

6. *You shall not commit adultery (*or rape).*

7. *You shall not show disrespect for your parents and elders.*

* Author addition

While no sacrifices were permitted within the colony, Melchizedek well knew how difficult it is to suddenly uproot long-established customs, and accordingly, had wisely offered these people the substitute of a sacrament of bread and wine for the older sacrifice of flesh and blood. It is of record, "Melchizedek, king of Salem, brought forth bread and wine."

But even this cautious innovation was not altogether successful; the various tribes all maintained auxiliary centers on the outskirts of Salem where they offered sacrifices and burnt offering. Even Abraham resorted to this barbarous practice after his victory over Cheldorlaomer; he simply did not feel quite at ease until he had offered a conventional sacrifice. And Melchizedek never did succeed in fully eradicating this proclivity to sacrifice from the religious practices of his followers, even of Abraham.

Like Jesus, Melchizedek attended strictly to the fulfillment of the mission of his bestowal. He did not attempt to reform the norms, to change the habits of the world, nor to promulgate even advanced sanitary practices or scientific truths. He came to achieve two tasks: to keep alive on earth the truth of the one God and to prepare the way for the subsequent mortal bestowal of a

Paradise Son of that Universal Father. (Whom we know today as Jesus of Nazareth).

Melchizedek taught elementary revealed truth at Salem for ninety-four years and during this time Abraham attended the Salem school three different times. He finally became a convert to the Salem teaching, becoming one of Melchizedek's most brilliant pupils and chief supporters." The Urantia Book 93:4.1-16

Personally, I look upon God as the Great Creator who created everything we see around us and is continually creating beings to enjoy what he created. I perceive that through His Children, He is reflecting all things true, beautiful, and good. It is us that make things out to be false, ugly, and bad if that is what we perceive. If we choose, we can grow up to become fabulous, creative, and ingenious.

It is important to learn about the part of the agreement where we believe in God's Promises.

It comes down to faith as being the ability to believe. Faith is the stage upon which those who believe act. Believing is what we do while we are having faith, and dreaming is us applying belief to our wishes and desires.

Wishing evolves into prayer. As a skill set, personal desires for a more abundant and progressive life reaches a level where the effects of wishing become more powerful as one develops the ability to pray.

You will do well by taking the following information from Paper 91 of The Urantia Book into account in your daily life, and applying prayer to your wish making.

The reason I am adding the following text to this treatise is that you deserve to hear what The Urantia Book reveals about the evolution of prayer and how it affects believing. There is more to prayer than we've been led to believe.

Paper 91 The Evolution of Prayer

PRAYER, as an agency of religion, evolved from previous non-religious monologue and dialogue expressions. With the attainment of self-consciousness by primitive man there occurred the inevitable corollary of other-consciousness, the dual potential of social response and God recognition.

The earliest prayer forms were not addressed to Deity. These expressions were much like what you would say to a friend as you entered upon some important undertaking, "Wish me luck." Primitive man was enslaved to magic; luck, good and bad, entered into all the affairs of life. At first, these luck petitions were monologues — just a kind of thinking out loud by the magic server. Next, these believers in luck would enlist the support of their friends and families, and presently some form of ceremony would be performed which included the whole clan or tribe.

When the concepts of ghosts and spirits evolved, these petitions became superhuman in address, and with the consciousness of gods, such expressions attained to the levels of genuine prayer. As an illustration of this, among certain Australian tribes primitive religious prayers antedated their belief in spirits and superhuman personalities.

The Toda tribe of India now observes this practice of praying to no one in particular, just as did the early peoples before the times of religious consciousness. Only, among the Todas, this represents a regression of their degenerating religion to this primitive level. The present-day rituals of the dairymen priests of the Todas do not represent a religious ceremony since these impersonal prayers do not contribute anything to the conservation or enhancement of any social, moral, or spiritual values.

Prereligious praying was part of the mana practices of the Melanesians, the oudah beliefs of the African Pygmies, and the manitou superstitions of the North American Indians. The Baganda tribes of Africa have only recently emerged from the mana level of prayer. In this early evolutionary confusion men pray to gods — local and national — to fetishes, amulets, ghosts, rulers, and to ordinary people.

1. Primitive Prayer

The function of early evolutionary religion is to conserve and augment the essential social, moral, and spiritual values which are slowly taking form. This mission of religion is not consciously observed by mankind, but it is chiefly effected by the function of prayer. The practice of prayer represents the unintended, but nonetheless personal and collective, effort of any group to secure (to actualize) this conservation of higher values. But for the safeguarding of prayer, all holy days would speedily revert to the status of mere holidays.

Religion and its agencies, the chief of which is prayer, are allied only with those values which have general social recognition, group approval. Therefore, when primitive man attempted to gratify his base emotions or to achieve unmitigated selfish ambitions, he was deprived of the consolation of religion and the assistance of prayer. If the individual sought to accomplish anything antisocial, he was obliged to seek the aid of nonreligious magic, resort to sorcerers, and thus be deprived of the assistance of prayer. Prayer, therefore, very early became a mighty promoter of social evolution, moral progress, and spiritual attainment.

But the primitive mind was neither logical nor consistent. Early men did not perceive that material things were not the province of prayer. These simple-minded souls reasoned that food, shelter, rain, game, and other material goods enhanced the social welfare, and therefore they began to pray for these physical blessings. While this constituted a perversion of prayer, it encouraged the effort to realize these material objectives by social and ethical actions. Such a prostitution of prayer, while debasing the spiritual values of a people, nevertheless directly elevated their economic, social, and ethical mores.

Prayer is only monologuous in the most primitive type of mind. It early becomes a dialogue and rapidly expands to the level of group worship. Prayer signifies that the premagical incantations of primitive religion have evolved to that level where the human mind recognizes the reality of beneficent powers or beings who are able to enhance social values and to augment moral ideals, and further, that these influences are superhuman and distinct from the ego of the self-conscious human and his fellow mortals. True prayer does not, therefore, appear until the agency of religious ministry is visualized as personal.

Prayer is little associated with animism, but such beliefs may exist alongside emerging religious sentiments. Many times, religion and animism have had entirely separate origins. (Animism is a doctrine that the vital principle of organic development is immaterial spirit; attribution of conscious life to nature or natural objects or belief in the existence of spirits imbued within any physical form.)*

*Author's addition

With those mortals who have not been delivered from the primitive bondage of fear, there is a real danger that all prayer may lead to a morbid sense of sin, unjustified convictions of guilt, real or fancied. But in modern times it is not likely that many will spend sufficient time at prayer to lead to this harmful brooding over their unworthiness or sinfulness. The dangers attendant upon the distortion and perversion of prayer consist in ignorance, superstition, crystallization, de-vitalization, materialism, and fanaticism.

2. Evolving Prayer

The first prayers were merely verbalized wishes, the expression of sincere desires. Prayer next became a technique of achieving spirit co-operation. And then it attained to the higher function of assisting religion in the conservation of all worth-while values.

Both prayer and magic arose as a result of man's adjustive reactions to Urantian environment. But aside from this generalized relationship, they have little in common. Prayer has always indicated positive action by the praying ego; it has been always psychic and sometimes spiritual. Magic has usually signified an attempt to manipulate reality without affecting the ego of the manipulator, the practitioner of magic. Despite their independent origins, magic and prayer have often been interrelated in their later stages of development. Magic has sometimes ascended by goal elevation from formulas through rituals and incantations to the threshold of true prayer. Prayer has sometimes become so materialistic that it has degenerated into a pseudomagical technique of avoiding the expenditure of that effort which is requisite for the solution of Urantian problems.

When man learned that prayer could not coerce the gods, then it became more of a petition, favor seeking. But the truest prayer is in reality a communion between man and his Maker.

The appearance of the sacrifice idea in any religion unfailingly detracts from the higher efficacy of true prayer in that men seek to substitute the offerings of material possessions for the offering of their own consecrated wills to the doing of the will of God.

When religion is divested of a personal God, its prayers translate to the levels of theology and philosophy. When the highest God concept of a religion is that of an impersonal Deity, such as in pantheistic idealism, although affording the basis for certain forms of mystic communion, it proves fatal to the potency of true prayer, which always stands for man's communion with a personal and superior being.

During the earlier times of racial evolution and even at the present time, in the day-by-day experience of the average mortal, prayer is very much a phenomenon of man's intercourse with his own subconscious. But there is also a domain of prayer wherein the intellectually alert and spiritually progressing individual attains more or less contact with the superconscious levels of the human mind, the domain of the indwelling Thought Adjuster. In addition, there is a definite spiritual phase of true prayer which concerns its reception and recognition by the spiritual forces of the universe, and which is entirely distinct from all human and intellectual association.

Prayer contributes greatly to the development of the religious sentiment of an evolving human mind. It is a mighty influence working to prevent isolation of personality.

Prayer represents one technique associated with the natural religions of racial evolution which also forms a part of the experiential values of the higher religions of ethical excellence, the religions of revelation.

3. Prayer and the Alter Ego

Children, when first learning to make use of language, are prone to think out loud, to express their thoughts in words, even if no one is present to hear them. With the dawn of creative imagination they evince a tendency to converse with imaginary companions. In this way a budding ego seeks to hold communion with a fictitious alter ego. By this technique the child early learns to convert his monologue conversations into pseudo dialogues in which this alter ego makes replies to his verbal thinking and wish expression. Very much of an adult's thinking is mentally carried on in conversational form.

The early and primitive form of prayer was much like the semimagical recitations of the present-day Toda tribe, prayers that were not addressed to anyone in particular. But such techniques of praying tend to evolve into the dialogue type of communication by the emergence of the idea of an alter ego. In time the alter-ego concept is exalted to a superior status of divine dignity, and prayer as an agency of religion has appeared. Through many phases and during long ages this primitive type of praying is destined to evolve before attaining the level of intelligent and truly ethical prayer.

As it is conceived by successive generations of praying mortals, the alter ego evolves up through ghosts, fetishes, and spirits to polytheistic gods, and eventually to the One God, a divine being embodying the highest ideals and the loftiest aspirations of the praying ego. And thus does prayer function as the most potent agency of religion in the conservation of the highest values and ideals of those who pray. From the moment of the conceiving of an alter ego to the appearance of the concept of a divine and heavenly Father, prayer is always a socializing, moralizing, and spiritualizing practice.

The simple prayer of faith evidences a mighty evolution in human experience whereby the ancient conversations with the fictitious symbol of the alter ego of primitive religion have become exalted to the level of communion with the spirit of the Infinite and to that of a bona fide consciousness of the reality of the eternal God and Paradise Father of all intelligent creation.

Aside from all that is superself in the experience of praying, it should be remembered that ethical prayer is a splendid way to elevate one's ego and reinforce the self for better living and higher attainment. Prayer induces the human ego to look both ways for help: for material aid to the subconscious reservoir of mortal experience, for inspiration and guidance to the superconscious borders of the contact of the material with the spiritual, with the Mystery Monitor. (i.e. AKA the Thought Adjuster.)*

*Author's addition

Prayer ever has been and ever will be a twofold human experience: a psychologic procedure interassociated with a spiritual technique. And these two functions of prayer can never be fully separated.

Enlightened prayer must recognize not only an external and personal God but also an internal and impersonal Divinity, the indwelling Adjuster. It is altogether fitting that man, when he prays, should strive to grasp the concept of the Universal Father on Paradise; but the more effective technique for most practical purposes will be to revert to the concept of a near-by alter ego, just as the primitive mind was wont to do, and then to recognize that the idea of this alter ego has evolved from a mere fiction to the truth of God's indwelling mortal man in the factual presence of the Adjuster so that man can talk face to face, as it were, with a real and genuine and divine alter ego that indwells him and is the very presence and essence of the living God, the Universal Father.

4. Ethical Praying

No prayer can be ethical when the petitioner seeks for selfish advantage over his fellows. Selfish and materialistic praying is incompatible with the ethical religions which are predicated on unselfish and divine love. All such unethical praying reverts to the primitive levels of pseudo magic and is unworthy of advancing civilizations and enlightened religions. Selfish praying transgresses the spirit of all ethics founded on loving justice.

Prayer must never be so prostituted as to become a substitute for action. All ethical prayer is a stimulus to action and a guide to the progressive striving for idealistic goals of superself-attainment.

In all your praying be fair; do not expect God to show partiality, to love you more than his other children, your friends, neighbors, even enemies. But the prayer of the natural or evolved religions is not at first ethical, as it is in the later revealed religions. All praying, whether individual or communal, may be either egoistic or altruistic. That is, the prayer may be centered upon the self or upon others. When the prayer seeks nothing for the one who prays nor anything for his fellows, then such attitudes of the soul tend to the levels of true worship. Egoistic prayers involve confessions and petitions and often consist in requests for material favors. Prayer is somewhat more ethical when it deals with forgiveness and seeks wisdom for enhanced self-control.

While the non-selfish type of prayer is strengthening and comforting, materialistic praying is destined to bring disappointment and disillusionment as advancing scientific discoveries demonstrate that man lives in a physical universe of law and order. The childhood of an individual or a race is characterized by primitive, selfish, and materialistic praying. And, to a certain extent, all such petitions are efficacious in that they unvaryingly lead to those efforts and exertions which are contributory to achieving the answers to such prayers. The real prayer of faith always contributes to the augmentation of the technique of living, even if such petitions are not worthy of spiritual recognition. But the spiritually advanced person should exercise great caution in attempting to discourage the primitive or immature mind regarding such prayers.

Remember, even if prayer does not change God, it very often effects great and lasting changes in the one who prays in faith and confident expectation. Prayer has been the ancestor of much peace of mind, cheerfulness, calmness, courage, self-mastery, and fair-mindedness in the men and women of the evolving races.

5. Social Repercussions of Prayer

In ancestor worship, prayer leads to the cultivation of ancestral ideals. But prayer, as a feature of Deity worship, transcends all other such practices since it leads to the cultivation of divine ideals. As the concept of the alter ego of prayer becomes supreme and divine, so are man's ideals accordingly elevated from mere human toward supernal and divine levels, and the result of all such praying is the enhancement of human character and the profound unification of human personality.

But prayer need not always be individual. Group or congregational praying is very effective in that it is highly socializing in its repercussions. When a group engages in community prayer for moral enhancement and spiritual uplift, such devotions are reactive upon the individuals composing the group; they are all made better because of participation. Even a whole city or an entire nation can be helped by such prayer devotions. Confession, repentance, and prayer have led individuals, cities, nations, and whole races to mighty efforts of reform and courageous deeds of valorous achievement.

If you truly desire to overcome the habit of criticizing some friend, the quickest and surest way of achieving such a change of attitude is to establish the habit of praying for that person every day of your life. But the social repercussions of such prayers are dependent largely on two conditions:

1. *The person who is prayed for should know that he is being prayed for.*

2. *The person who prays should come into intimate social contact with the person for whom he is praying.*

Prayer is the technique whereby, sooner or later, every religion becomes institutionalized. And in time prayer becomes associated with numerous secondary agencies, some helpful, others decidedly deleterious, such as priests, holy books, worship rituals, and ceremonials.

But the minds of greater spiritual illumination should be patient with, and tolerant of, those less endowed intellects that crave symbolism for the mobilization of their feeble spiritual insight. The strong must not look with disdain upon the weak. Those who are God-conscious without symbolism must not deny the grace-ministry of the symbol to those who find it difficult to worship Deity and to revere truth, beauty, and goodness without form and ritual. In prayerful worship, most mortals envision some symbol of the object-goal of their devotions.

6. The Province of Prayer

Prayer, unless in liaison with the will and actions of the personal spiritual forces and material supervisors of a realm, can have no direct effect upon one's physical environment. While there is a very definite limit to the province of the petitions of prayer, such limits do not equally apply to the faith of those who pray.

Prayer is not a technique for curing real and organic diseases, but it has contributed enormously to the enjoyment of abundant health and to the cure of numerous mental, emotional, and nervous ailments. And even in actual bacterial disease, prayer has many times added to the efficacy of other remedial procedures. Prayer has turned many an irritable and complaining invalid into a paragon of patience and made him an inspiration to all other human sufferers.

No matter how difficult it may be to reconcile the scientific doubtings regarding the efficacy of prayer with the ever-present urge to seek help and guidance from divine sources, never forget that the sincere prayer of faith is a mighty force for the promotion of personal happiness, individual self-control, social harmony, moral progress, and spiritual attainment.

Prayer, even as a purely human practice, a dialogue with one's alter ego, constitutes a technique of the most efficient approach to the realization of those reserve powers of human nature which are stored and conserved in the unconscious realms of the human mind. Prayer is a sound psychologic practice, aside from its religious implications and its spiritual significance. It is a fact of human experience that most persons, if sufficiently hard pressed, will pray in some way to some source of help.

Do not be so slothful as to ask God to solve your difficulties, but never hesitate to ask him for wisdom and spiritual strength to guide and sustain you while you yourself resolutely and courageously attack the problems at hand.

Prayer has been an indispensable factor in the progress and preservation of religious civilization, and it still has mighty contributions to make to the further enhancement and spiritualization of society if those who pray will only do so in the light of scientific facts, philosophic wisdom, intellectual sincerity, and spiritual faith. Pray as Jesus taught his disciples — honestly, unselfishly, with fairness, and without doubting.

But the efficacy of prayer in the personal spiritual experience of the one who prays is in no way dependent on such a worshiper's intellectual understanding, philosophic acumen, social level, cultural status, or other mortal acquirements. The psychic and spiritual concomitants of the prayer of faith are immediate, personal, and experiential. There is no other technique whereby every man, regardless of all other mortal accomplishments, can so effectively and immediately approach the threshold of that realm wherein he can communicate with his Maker, where the creature contacts with the reality of the Creator, with the indwelling Thought Adjuster.

7. Mysticism, Ecstasy, and Inspiration

Mysticism, as the technique of the cultivation of the consciousness of the presence of God, is altogether praiseworthy, but when such practices lead to social isolation and culminate in religious fanaticism, they are all but reprehensible. Altogether too frequently that which the overwrought mystic evaluates as divine inspiration is the uprisings of his own deep mind. The contact of the mortal mind with its indwelling Adjuster, while often favored by devoted meditation, is more frequently facilitated by wholehearted and loving service in unselfish ministry to one's fellow creatures.

The great religious teachers and the prophets of past ages were not extreme mystics. They were God-knowing men and women who best served their God by unselfish ministry to their fellow mortals. Jesus often took his apostles away by themselves for short periods to engage in meditation and prayer, but for the most part he kept them in service-contact with the multitudes. The soul of man requires spiritual exercise as well as spiritual nourishment.

Religious ecstasy is permissible when resulting from sane antecedents, but such experiences are more often the outgrowth of purely emotional influences than a manifestation of deep spiritual character. Religious persons must not regard every vivid psychologic presentiment and every intense emotional experience as a divine revelation or a spiritual communication. Genuine spiritual ecstasy is usually associated with great outward calmness and almost perfect emotional control. But true prophetic vision is a superpsychologic presentiment. Such visitations are not pseudo hallucinations, neither are they trancelike ecstasies.

The human mind may perform in response to so-called inspiration when it is sensitive either to the uprisings of the subconscious or to the stimulus of the super-conscious. In either case it appears to the individual that such augmentations of the content of consciousness are more or less foreign. Unrestrained mystical enthusiasm and rampant religious ecstasy are not the credentials of inspiration, supposedly divine credentials.

The practical test of all these strange religious experiences of mysticism, ecstasy, and inspiration is to observe whether these phenomena cause an individual:

1. To enjoy better and more complete physical health.

2. To function more efficiently and practically in his mental life.

3. More fully and joyfully to socialize his religious experience.

4. More completely to spiritualize his day-by-day living while faithfully discharging the commonplace duties of routine mortal existence.

5. To enhance his love for, and appreciation of, truth, beauty, and goodness.

6. To conserve currently recognized social, moral, ethical, and spiritual values.

7. To increase his spiritual insight — God-consciousness.

But prayer has no real association with these exceptional religious experiences. When prayer becomes overmuch aesthetic, when it consists almost exclusively in beautiful and blissful contemplation of paradisiacal divinity, it loses much of its socializing influence and tends toward mysticism and the isolation of its devotees. There is a certain danger associated with overmuch private praying which is corrected and prevented by group praying, community devotions.

8. Praying as a Personal Experience

There is a truly spontaneous aspect to prayer, for primitive man found himself praying long before he had any clear concept of a God. Early man was wont to pray in two diverse situations: When in dire need, he experienced the impulse to reach out for help; and when jubilant, he indulged the impulsive expression of joy.

Prayer is not an evolution of magic; they each arose independently. Magic was an attempt to adjust Deity to conditions; prayer is the effort to adjust the personality to the will of Deity. True prayer is both moral and religious; magic is neither.

Prayer may become an established custom; many pray because others do. Still others pray because they fear something direful may happen if they do not offer their regular supplications.

To some individuals prayer is the calm expression of gratitude; to others, a group expression of praise, social devotions; sometimes it is the imitation of another's religion, while in true praying it is the sincere and trusting communication of the spiritual nature of the creature with the anywhere presence of the spirit of the Creator.

(I am so joyful to be able to sense the presence of the Creator in my daily life. I feel I am doing what many others wish they could do. To be able to communicate with an incredible Intelligence that knows all things.)

Prayer may be a spontaneous expression of God-consciousness or a meaningless recitation of theological formulas. It may be the ecstatic praise of a God-knowing soul or the slavish obeisance of a fear-ridden mortal. It is sometimes the pathetic expression of spiritual craving and sometimes the blatant shouting of pious phrases. Prayer may be joyous praise or a humble plea for forgiveness.

Prayer may be the childlike plea for the impossible or the mature entreaty for moral growth and spiritual power. A petition may be for daily bread or may embody a wholehearted yearning to find God and to do his will. It may be a wholly selfish request or a true and magnificent gesture toward the realization of unselfish brotherhood.

(Lately, during the COVID19 pandemic, we are finding a community of voices expressing care and concern for the health and welfare of each other. It's truly amazing to watch unfold.)

Prayer may be an angry cry for vengeance or a merciful intercession for one's enemies. It may be the expression of a hope of changing God or the powerful technique of changing one's self. It may be the cringing plea of a lost sinner before a supposedly stern Judge or the joyful expression of a liberated son of the living and merciful heavenly Father.

(There are only two directions in life. Becoming more of, or becoming less of. We are either focused on the joy of belonging to God or being held ransom by somebody's idea of sin in a world of judgment. It's up to us as to whether we see stars or bars.)

Modern man is perplexed by the thought of talking things over with God in a purely personal way. Many have abandoned regular praying; they only pray when under unusual pressure — in emergencies. Man should be unafraid to talk to God, but only a spiritual child would undertake to persuade, or presume to change, God.

But real praying does attain reality. Even when the air currents are ascending, no bird can soar except by outstretched wings. Prayer elevates man because it is a technique of progressing by the utilization of the ascending spiritual currents of the universe.

Genuine prayer adds to spiritual growth, modifies attitudes, and yields that satisfaction which comes from communion with divinity. It is a spontaneous outburst of God-consciousness.

God answers man's prayer by giving him an increased revelation of truth, an enhanced appreciation of beauty, and an augmented concept of goodness. Prayer is a subjective gesture, but it contacts with mighty objective realities on the spiritual levels of human experience; it is a meaningful reach by the human for super-human values. It is the most potent spiritual-growth stimulus.

Words are irrelevant to prayer; they are merely the intellectual channel in which the river of spiritual supplication may chance to flow. The word value of a prayer is purely autosuggestive in private devotions and sociosuggestive in group devotions. God answers the soul's attitude, not the words.

Prayer is not a technique of escape from conflict but rather a stimulus to growth in the very face of conflict. Pray only for values, not things; for growth, not for gratification.

9. Conditions of Effective Prayer

If you would engage in effective praying, you should bear in mind the laws of prevailing petitions:

1. You must qualify as a potent prayer by sincerely and courageously facing the problems of universe reality. You must possess cosmic stamina.

2. *You must have honestly exhausted the human capacity for human adjustment. You must have been industrious.*

3. *You must surrender every wish of mind and every craving of soul to the transforming embrace of spiritual growth. You must have experienced an enhancement of meanings and an elevation of values.*

4. *You must make a wholehearted choice of the divine will. You must obliterate the dead center of indecision.*

5. *You not only recognize the Father's will and choose to do it, but you have effected an unqualified consecration, and a dynamic dedication, to the actual doing of the Father's will.*

6. *Your prayer will be directed exclusively for divine wisdom to solve the specific human problems encountered in the Paradise ascension — the attainment of divine perfection.*

7. *And you must have faith — living faith.*

[*Presented by the Chief of the Urantia Midwayers.*]
The Urantia Book: *Paper 91*

The last few paragraphs express the need for us to be able to listen to God's instructions. We must be willing to hear the voice of spirit so we can implement the solutions to our problems. We must be able to listen to the directions being given to us, in order to effect the changes in the world we would like to see. We are in charge of our list of perceptions, inclinations, and meditations.

Believe

It's easier to understand "When You Wish upon a Star" if you first believe in God; that there is such an entity, idea, ideal or thing such as God, an Almighty Lord of Hosts!

I tell myself the story that there is a God, and that this one and only "Supreme Being" is personally accessible and user-friendly to me.

I like to tell people, *"God's throwing a party today and you've been invited! In fact, you are the guest of honor: so please help us open the present."*

The function of belief, I found, is a series of mental events with sub-routines of consequential thinking, decisions, and actions.

Believing in something means "to understand something with all the bells and whistles and rhymes and reasons of why some particular something is, or could be, or should be." When you are thinking, you are in the process of believing. Consequential thinking is the ability to perceive that one thing leads to another and all the dominos fall as a result of the initial tipping of the first block of paying attention.

Most of us spend the majority of our time justifying whether something is an illusion or reality. We spend our time judging. And then, the universe jumps in to show us examples of what we are thinking about; reflecting back to us what we are spending our time believing in, like a mirror. We rehearse reasons to believe that *'such and such'* is and entertain psychodramas of how *'so and so'* is; and as we so believe, so it becomes, even more so as we energize those beliefs with our emotions of bliss or anger.

"Mind is the Master power that moulds and makes, And Man is Mind, and evermore he takes The tool of Thought, and, shaping what he wills, Brings forth a thousand joys, a thousand ills: He thinks in secret, and it comes to pass: Environment is but his looking-glass."
— *James Allen, "As a Man Thinketh"*

"There is a thinking stuff which in its original form permeates, penetrates, and fills the interspaces of the Universe. A thought in this substance produces the thing that is imaged by that thought."
— *Wallace Wattles, "The Science of Getting Rich"*

Belief is the plot we design, and as emotional actors, we commit ideas to action in the process of believing in our dream.

"And, if your heart is in your dreams, No request is too extreme." — Leigh Harline and Ned Washington, *"When You Wish Upon a Star"*

When believing in the story you are listening to right now, whether you are telling the story or someone else is, you're the only one that's making sense of it. Hopefully the plot you're designing can stand up to "your" criticism, now and in the future.

Film celebrity, Jim Carrey, was speaking at a high school graduation commencement ceremony when he told the students, "It's all about letting the Universe know what you want, and working toward it while letting go of how it comes to pass. Your job is not to figure out how it is going to happen for you, but to open the door in your head, and when the door opens in real life just walk through it. Don't worry if you miss your cue because there's always more doors opening, they keep opening." You are guiding yourself into potential timelines according to your attitudes, decisions, musings, judgments, and considerations. Tell the Universe what you want.

The greatest story you will ever hear is the one you tell yourself. What you believe in is also what you hope to achieve. What you hope to achieve becomes the reference point of your future personality, wrapped in memories, as your daily life oozes from your soul into the universe at hand. Your feel for life; your love for life, or your experience of life, is in the meanings held between you and your loved ones; friends, acquaintances, co-workers, clients, and customers; Star and the Universe reflects back to you accordingly.

The story you tell yourself is filled with life dramas and interaction, as well as interruptions with others. The story we've been brought up to believe in all along, continues until our skill of believing is so upgraded through personal mastery of thought that we can now believe in possible, hopeful worlds. Thinking is a mental function; a skill we develop, practice, and polish to improve our mental acuity and perception; sharpness of creativity and insightfulness. Brilliance!

"I am continuously thinking positive thoughts that make me happy, successful, and prosperous. I am also using more and more of my mind, and using it in such a special manner that I am becoming more and more of a genius each and every successive day."
— Thomas D. Willhite, PSI Seminars

This statement was impressed upon me by Thomas Willhite during the seminar he offered to the public in the 1970's for uplifting the dynamics of the human family. I memorized this idiom and found myself using it as a tool for sculpting my world. I also learned that skill development connects the attainment of four levels of achievement.

The first level is unconscious incompetence. You don't know that you can't do something. The second level is conscious incompetence. You find out that you can't do something, like tying shoelaces or playing a guitar.

Then comes level three; conscious competence. This is the level where you apply yourself by learning how to perform the task you wish to express. This level includes all your successes and mistakes.

Finally, level four is unconscious competence. This is when you have achieved mastery and can just do something almost without much thought to it. You can just do it.

There are very few great thinkers in our world. The effort to control thought comes at the expense of having to pay attention long enough so that the thought we are thinking gets impressed upon the substance of reality – embossed upon the Universe at large.

Whatever the mind can conceive, and believe, it can achieve! — *Napoleon Hill, "Think and Grow Rich"*

The process of believing starts with a wish. Then it becomes a dream. Then it becomes a desire. Then it morphs into spending a lot of time thinking about it. Then it turns into an obsession. You then determine what you're willing to do to make your dream come true.

All this time you are telling a story. You start to write about it and tell close friends what you're up to and then keep them in the dark until the wish becomes a reality. Burning desire will convince you that this is what you must do today to bring your dream to pass.

This is the process of "...*following God's instructions.*"

Every step closer to your dream will reveal the next step after that. You will eventually climb your successes like a ladder, to abundance. Put your thoughts in order to arrange the life you choose for yourself and your loved ones. You can do it. Figure it out.

Dreaming is a Skill of Believing/ Thinking/Imagining

Don't become an intellectual giant, only to fetter the skills you've mastered, in obedience to theologies and cultural tradition; doing so keeps you from helping the culture at large. Step up and help advance the world in reflecting truth, beauty, and goodness for yourself and your children.

Develop mastery over your imagination and it will set you free; not doing so will lead you to setting yourself in bondage. See your imagination as the tool with which you view the screen of your mind; the silver screen in your brain upon which is portrayed the images and dramas you conjure, and conjecture. You are the story teller; the film director of YOUR life. If the story you were brought up to believe in no longer serves you, you are free to change that story. There is no law in the universe that says anyone must endure pain, suffering, or terrorism. Go beyond! Be beyond!

With your imagination, you will either see stars or bars. With your imagination, you will describe to yourself that things are turning out as dark, sumptuous red roses or, that everything is quickly going to hell in a red hot hand basket. Your imagination is the "believing" tool with which you make sense of things, and with which you receive feedback. It's what you worry with. Your imagination helps you solve your problems. Visualize the movie of your life, the one you are now observing, positively.

Spend some time dreaming.

Imagine what it would be like if your dreams came true. Imagine how things could be.

When you wish upon a star, your dreams come true. Picture your life as it will be when everything has come true; when your dreams have become a reality, to your liking and everywhere you look, you find what you need when you need it. Resources become available. Parking spots appear out of the blue. Checks arrive in the mail from everywhere. Traffic lights turn green in a timely manner. You find that you would dare to give everyone a piece of your mind and you don't. You begin to build a future that can stand up to your criticism. You become so strong that you can put other people first.

Dreaming is a full-time job. It demands that you become proficient in sequential thinking. It suffers you to envision cause and effect. Dreaming is one of the most sacred events you will ever enact in your life. Your dreams will come true when you allow them to become visible if only to yourself at first.

You have the ability to create thoughts in your mind that can reflect three very important parts of life: the ability to discern truth, beauty, and goodness; the ability to appreciate truth, beauty, and goodness; and the ability to promote truth, beauty, and goodness.

Serendipity shows up as a response by God to your dreams. You don't think God is listening? God is closer than you think. God is closer to you than you've ever been led to believe. In fact, God is listening to the same things you are right now and feeling every feeling you feel right along with you. Only you and God have the privilege of knowing what you feel and think about.

God gifted you with free will. You are free to think of whatever you wish to think of, and use the gifts of conjecture and supposition. Suppose I were to do this. Then would this other happen?

If I were to spend my time, believing something is possible, would I then be able to 'continue' to believe that it's possible? Seem like a lot of work? Thinking will be the hardest work you will ever perform.

Spontaneous events and serendipity occur when we follow our dreams. But you won't get to find that out until you push the button and let go of something; of someone standing in your way for instance. When you climb the ladder, you must first let go of one rung of the ladder for a next, higher rung. Don't be hesitant. You can use one hand for stability, reliability, and sustenance, while you reach for the next rung with the other. Uncertainty will become sublime.

When you search for a new shore, you must first leave the harbor of your birth. You have all the necessary facilities for putting your dreams into production.

Appreciate that God is the only one with access to your thoughts and feelings, besides you. This allows you to use the adjutant mind spirits of intuition, understanding, knowledge, courage, counsel, including worship and wisdom as your super powers. These superpowers will get you through the toughest parts of being a co-creator, designing dreams that have never been done before: by finding a need and filling it. You can learn more about these "super powers" in The Urantia Book: The Seven Adjutant Mind Spirits.

My friend, waste no thought in useless speculation. Secure the wondrous blessings of optimism. Zero in on the concept of focused liberty for yourself first, and then help your neighbor do the same, so that you both can live in a community of like-minded, liberated individuals living in the wealth of love, laughter, and life.

Liberty is the ability to have what you want, when you want to have it; say what you want to say, when you want to say it; go where you want to go, when you want to go there, for as long as you want and with whomever or not. But, it is not something we are automatically born with. We must secure this blessing for ourselves as we establish a life for our self.

When asking God for promises, as we find ourselves doing periodically, we are usually faced with uncertainties that are new and unmatched in our personal histories. We must remember, at the time, to suspend judgment. We must remember that we personally don't know it all and that uncertainty of the outcome of some things is okay!

Doubt is negative believing, negative dreaming. When you find yourself entertaining doubt, stop; turn yourself around! Identify to yourself that you're entertaining thoughts of doubt and begin to describe the opposite of the doubt you are viewing. Describe to yourself what it is you do want; not what it is you don't want. As you can describe what you do want, then that is what will be created.

If you can believe, then you can do great things. If you can believe in God's promises, then you will do even greater things.

God Promises

When you were young, were you ever taught how to pray? Were you ever taught how to ask God for promises? Were you ever taught how to petition God for a dream to come true?

I've come to realize that I have this magnificently divine being hovering closely; quietly within my mind. Once upon a time, it patiently waited for me to awaken and enjoy its most wondrous presence! For some, this hasn't happened yet.

Simple trust in the One and Only God is all that is required for our salvation; for us to permit the spark of Life and Light to enter our being. There is no need to believe in paying ransom for some perceived transgression or betrayal through default of some original sin, by some original son. Recall that there is/was first original innocence; and God the Father promises you haven't defaulted on anything that would cause you to forfeit your life or become separated from Him. This applies to all your brothers and sisters as well.

"For I am persuaded, that neither death, nor life, nor angels, nor princes, nor powers, nor things present, nor things to come, nor height, nor depth, nor any other creature, shall be able to separate us from the love of God." Romans 8:38-39

God is within you at this very moment, loving you and caring for you from within your mind and in your heart. The Father/Mother God is hanging out with you at the control panel on the **G**reat **O**bservation **D**eck of your mind. Things you entertain in your mind are exposed to the one person you would want to share them with, God. Know that God is within you. God is your soul mate. Because of this, you should never feel lonely.

The highest concept of God that we can have is that of a loving Father; a loving Mother. Enjoy having this being residing within your mind; inside your soul. God cares a great deal about you, but you can't hear God because of the noise inside your head. There's the noise of too many psychodramas and too many superstitions, opinions, and distractions keeping you from hearing. Learn to listen. "Be still and know God!"

An example of asking God for something would be like, proposing that God promises that you develop the ability to listen; to learn to read, for instance, or to become literate and graduate with top honors from a university.

We each need to learn how to make promises with God and then add the following words at the end of each petition, "…or, something better according to Your intelligent and wise will."

The most powerful prayer one can pray is to ask God how to pray, and then through experience, learn how to ask God for promises; to be able to identify and discern what's worthy of God's attention. God awaits our requests and proposals as any concerned father or mother would… for their beloved children.

I've requested promises from God. I will share them with you. For instance, I've asked God to make my financial affairs prosperous, and I've learned how to have patient gratitude as promises are being fulfilled. Some of my dreams get put on the back burner as I concentrate on the skillet of present concerns.

Mind you I don't wish to be rich just for the sake of being rich… I like the idea of what money can do. I have therefore become wealthy with available resources capable of producing great results. I'm not into just accumulating money, but using resources to make our world a better place for all. Money is like manure, it really isn't any good until its spread around. Upon my inevitable death I would rather be able to say, "I've spent $350 million dollars," than "I have $350 million in some bank," — because, guess what? You can't take it with you. And, anyone inheriting it wouldn't understand all the effort it took to create it in the first place. They wouldn't appreciate it… as much.

Like you've heard before, it's not money but the love of money which brings forth ills and evil. Money itself is both a divine and moral means of us being of service to each other.

God wants us to learn how to be hosts and hostesses, like God; to give without thought of return. That is why God is so often referred to as the Lord of Hosts. So, practice being the best host you can be. Host incredible parties, inviting those whom you feel would join you and see life as a most fabulous party.

Children should/could be reared in the education of promise fulfillment. They must learn "the system" of how to make requests for things they want; things that are desirable.

They must learn how to state requests without fear of denial, belittlement, or retribution, but with enthusiasm. Children must learn how consequential thinking helps in making decisions and then about keeping those decisions made.

In reading The Urantia Book, I've discovered what I feel is one of the most awesome promises ever made, and fulfilled, to humanity 2,000 years ago; the promise that the Spirit of Truth would be poured out upon all flesh. According to the Urantia Book, I discern and believe this happened on May 18th in the year 30 C.E., the day of Pentecost. Jesus speaking:

"Presently the Spirit of Truth shall be poured out upon all flesh, and it will live among men (*and women) and teach all men (*and women), even as I now live among you and speak to you the words of truth. And this Spirit of Truth, speaking for the spiritual endowments of your souls, will help you to know that you are the sons (*and

daughters) of God. It will unfailingly bear witness with the Father's indwelling presence, your spirit, then dwelling in all men (*and women) as it now dwells in some, telling you that you are in reality the sons (*and daughters) of God." The Urantia Book (1642.2) 146:3.6
*Author's addition

This Spirit of Truth is recognizable by men and women as it appears for each. Some people are still asleep and recognize not this Spirit of Truth. No matter. This doesn't mean they are devoid of the Spirit of Truth; it only means they have not yet awakened to its presence. We can pray (petition the Father) that our fellows soon waken from their slumber and learn to recognize the truth of the present family of humankind.

We must allow ourselves to be role models of this belief to others and be excited about the assurances of this promise; that we indeed are all brothers and sisters of the one and only hue-man family; hue-man meaning colorful people, or God Man.

The good news Jesus spoke of to everyone was the message of the Fatherhood of God and the Brotherhood of Men, and back then, 2,000 years ago, people received this "Good News" with great joy and immense comfort.

This is the story we must believe in and share with others, in order for there to be Peace on Earth and Goodwill toward All Men and Women.

If more people would have just kept His message alive from 2,000 years ago; if we could have just stuck to this main principle, this main theme of instruction, the one offered by Jesus, oh my, how different our world would look today.

I must say, the most fun part of my journey through life so far has been the awareness of God's presence daily. I have this very cool person with me that inspires me to believe that all things and thoughts are possible. This person has helped me listen to a higher voice from a supernatural level of existence. I'm getting to experience the presence of God in my life.

I'm getting to enjoy the conscious awareness of the presence of the personality of God. I don't have to wait till I "go to heaven" before I reach this fullness of human maturity.

I get to hang out with God.

I love you God. God, I love you! You, God, I love!

Makes me want to sing. Laa…

Following God's Instructions

Mind you, instructions from God, sometimes show up when we least expect them. A certain quality and sincerity of the petitioner seems to matter as instructions randomly appear either as insight, premonitions, visions or oddly occurring flashes and/or 'previews of coming attractions.' There may be something someone says that strikes a chord in us.

There was once a young man who set out to accomplish one dream, and yet a different dream came to pass which turned out better than the one he was hoping for.

The Young Man Who Was Afraid

While they were up in the mountains, Jesus had a long talk with a young man who was fearful and downcast. Failing to derive comfort and courage from association with his fellows, this youth had sought the solitude of the hills; he had grown up with a feeling of helplessness and inferiority. These natural tendencies had been augmented by numerous difficult circumstances which the lad had encountered as he grew up, notably, the loss of his father when he was twelve years of age. As they met, Jesus said: "Greetings, my friend! why so downcast on such a beautiful day? If something has happened to distress you, perhaps I can in some manner assist you. At any rate it affords me real pleasure to proffer my services."

The young man was disinclined to talk, and so Jesus made a second approach to his soul, saying: "I understand you come up in these hills to get away from folks; so, of course, you do not want to talk with me, but I would like to know whether you are familiar with these hills; do you know the direction of the trails? And, perchance, could you inform me as to the best route to Phenix?" Now this youth was very familiar with these mountains, and he really became much interested in telling Jesus the way to Phenix, so much so that he marked out all the trails on the ground and fully explained every detail. But he was startled and made curious when Jesus, after saying goodbye and making as if he were taking leave, suddenly turned to him, saying: "I well know you wish to be left alone with your disconsolation; but it would be neither kind nor fair for me to receive such generous help from you as to how best to find my way to Phenix and then unthinkingly to go away from you without making the least effort to answer your appealing request for help and guidance regarding the best route to the goal of destiny which you seek in your heart while you tarry here on the mountainside. As you so well know the trails to Phenix, having traversed them many times, so do I well know the way to the city of your disappointed hopes and thwarted ambitions. And since you have asked me for help, I will not disappoint you." The youth was almost overcome, but he managed to stammer out, "But — I did not ask you for anything — " And Jesus, laying a gentle hand on his shoulder, said: "No, son, not with words but with longing looks did you appeal to my heart. My boy, to one who loves his fellows there is an eloquent appeal for help in your countenance of discouragement and despair. Sit down with me while I tell you of the service trails and happiness highways which lead from the sorrows of self to the joys of loving activities in the brotherhood of men and in the service of the God of heaven."

By this time, the young man very much desired to talk with Jesus, and he knelt at his feet imploring Jesus to help him, to show him the way of escape from his world of personal sorrow and defeat.

Said Jesus to him, "My friend, arise! Stand up like a man! You may be surrounded with small enemies and be retarded by many obstacles, but the big things and the real things of this world and the universe are on your side. The sun rises every morning to salute you just as it does the most powerful and prosperous man on earth. Look — you have a strong body and powerful muscles — your physical equipment is better than the average. Of course, it is just about useless while you sit out here on the mountainside and grieve over your misfortunes, real and fancied. But you could do great things with your body if you would hasten off to where great things are waiting to be done. You are trying to run away from your unhappy self, but it cannot be done. You and your problems of living are real; you cannot escape them as long as you live. But look again, your mind is clear and capable. Your strong body has an intelligent mind to direct it. Set your mind at work to solve its problems; teach your intellect to work for you; refuse longer to be dominated by fear like an unthinking animal.

Your mind should be your most courageous ally in the solution of your life problems rather than your being, as you have been, its abject fear-slave and the bond-servant of depression and defeat. But most valuable of all, your potential of real achievement is the spirit which lives within you, and which will stimulate and inspire your mind to control itself and activate the body if you will release it from the fetters of fear and thus enable your spiritual nature to begin your deliverance from the evils of inaction by the power-presence of living faith. And then, forthwith, will this faith vanquish fear of men by the compelling presence of that new and all-dominating love of your fellows which will so soon fill your soul to overflowing because of the consciousness which has been born in your heart that you are a child of God."

"This day, my son, you are to be reborn, re-established as a man of faith, courage, and devoted service to man, for God's sake. And when you become so readjusted to life within yourself, you become likewise readjusted to the universe; you have been born again — born of the spirit — and henceforth will your whole life become one of victorious accomplishment.

Trouble will invigorate you; disappointment will spur you on; difficulties will challenge you; and obstacles will stimulate you. Arise, young man! Say farewell to the life of cringing fear and fleeing cowardice. Hasten back to duty and live your life in the flesh as a son of God, a mortal dedicated to the ennobling service of man on earth and destined to the superb and eternal service of God in eternity." The Urantia Book 130:6:1-4

So this lad had gone up to wander the trails of this mountain, and "happened" to be there at the same time as was Jesus, and was blessed by this chance meeting, unsuspecting that this person talking with him was the Paradise Creator Son of the local Universe.

In learning how to follow God's instructions, we must be willing to look for the truth, beauty, and goodness in everything, especially when we are faced with what appears to be negative situations.

Everything we attract causes us to grow, which means that ultimately everything is for our own good.

When we recognize something isn't working, it's important that we fess up to that understanding and be willing to give something else a try. Adjusting ourselves to new paths and direction requires adopting new habits of quality and strengths of character, and that these qualities are always exactly what we need to acquire in order to enjoy gratitude for the great things ahead in life. Refer to my popular book *"The Be Attitudes, A Catalog of Life and Light,"* for an example of a vast menu of attitudes to select from - a wardrobe of positivity and character building strengths. *thebeattitudes.com/*

Instructions give us access to the resources we need to use to make our lives better; to be rich in resources. The ability to follow these instructions means we must be highly teachable and instructable and then to act. We must be Meek!

The meek; the teachable, shall inherit the world. In contrast, those who already "know it all" are doomed to live in a world that no longer exists and then marvel as life begins to fall apart and feel like an illusion.

"I will instruct you and teach you in the way which you shalt go: I will guide you with my eyes." Psalm 32:8

Find a need and fill it.

In the past, I've spent a lot of time telling various people that my job was to help make other people's dreams come true. My job was to ask what they wanted done, and I would help them make it happen. These wishes or dreams usually concerned things about their house; like fixing a light or replacing a garbage disposal, or painting or replacing things that wore out over time. I was what you would call a "Handy Jane."

That effort taught me that no matter what things people wanted done, I could do it. Most things were easy to accomplish. And when it came time to install new stuff, there would inevitably be an owner's manual, or some set of installation instructions, included in the box the item came in, that would show how to do most anything without having to attend trade school or advanced classes. Plus, these days all sorts of instructions can be "Googled."

My self-made occupation worked for me for a time and provided a means of survival and maintenance for my life. I was soon to be overtaken by an urge to start working on making "my" dreams come true. I thought,

"If I were to apply this much effort given to others on my dreams… how much further along toward my dreams would I be?"

I was going through the various levels of skill development with my life. At the time I didn't know that I could change things if I wanted. I discerned I was feeling dissatisfied with my life and I felt there must be more. My plea turned into a wish and then my wish turned into a desire and then my desire turned into an obsession.

I've had tutors come into my life that spoke of many issues needing to be addressed. I considered them to be my teachers, my guides and gurus. I found out my life was about to become incredible, as everything started to coalesce: uniting as a whole. So I ventured forth and became successful and prosperous.

"Maturity is becoming aware of the responsibility, or response ability, of our mind. Becoming a master of our thinking and our feelings is the hallmark of a matured human being."
— Thomas D. Willhite *PSI Seminars*

Being able to follow directions makes us the best possible leader, employee or associate and partner available. As we learn to think, to believe in, and more specifically, follow instructions, we gain great insight and can see and offer wisdom to others.

Some instructions are subsumed by the body's autonomic nervous system. Imagine trying to regulate your heartbeat by conscious thought. Most of us would just end up dead. We need to upgrade our thinking.

Following instructions is like following grandma's recipe for great oatmeal cookies or following a formula, or reviewing the work of a mathematician; reading the directions on the box or in the package. Enacting any procedure as stated would be considered "following the instructions."

Each time we obtain a new appliance we need to read the owner's manual. We live in a day and age when we've become subject to tutorials. We learn how each device works. Yet, we don't have to know why or how something works. We simply need to know what it is we want done and then do it. They who know why always employ they who know how and don't necessarily need to know how them self. We learn what each device does, become familiar with its parts and how to make it work for us, but we don't need to learn how it works.

So, what's the payoff for not only believing but also following instructions, you may ask? What's in it for you? Well, you get to have your wishes granted! You get to have your dreams come true! You get to truly enjoy living in heaven on earth! Ultimately, in the long run, you get to be immortal! And, we all get to have all that we sincerely want, no matter how long it takes or however many life times it requires.

"But every human being should remember: Many ambitions to excel which tantalize mortals in the flesh will not persist with these same mortals in the (afterlife) *morontia and spirit careers. The ascending morontians learn to socialize their former purely selfish longings and egoistic ambitions. Nevertheless, those things which you so earnestly longed to do on earth and which circumstances so persistently denied you, if, after acquiring true mota insight in the morontia career, you still desire to do, then will you most certainly be granted every opportunity fully to satisfy your long-cherished desires."* The Urantia Book 44:8.4

Look around. Jesus told us "the Kingdom of Heaven is at hand." We are already in heaven, some just can't see it yet, and are still asleep in their consciousness of God's presence.

Give without thought of return. Aspire to greatness, especially through being of service to all. Experience the bliss in being of service to your fellows.

Jesus taught that his kingdom was not of this world, and that all men, being the sons of God, should find liberty and freedom in the spiritual joy of the fellowship of the brotherhood of loving service in this new kingdom of the truth of the heavenly Father's love.

In Genesis 1:28 we were blessed by God to, *"Be fertile and multiply."* THRIVE! In other words, this garden given to us is vast in resources, available for us to enjoy. Feast upon that, which has been so richly prepared for you. Enjoy the company of each other and with your brothers and sisters, your loved ones; enjoy what you can so richly share between each of you.

Some esoteric sample instructions would be as follows:
- Love one another as I have so loved you.
- Give without thought of return.
- Be ye perfect even as I am.
- Control your tongue.
- To think is to create.
- Take the talents you were born with, and polish them into skills.
- Get paid in direct proportion to the services you render to others.
- To those who would be first, learn to be last.
- Your fellow human is not just your brother; he is you.
- Be so strong that you can put other's first.
- If you don't like something, be willing to change it.
- The inferior must always give way to the superior – although for a period they must live side by side.
- According to your faith, be it done unto you.
- Darkness cannot exist in the presence of light, so go forward on purpose and whatever you need, will be there when you get there.

- Don't let fear stand in the way of a dream coming true.
- Face the light and the shadows fall behind you.

I discovered that what helps me the most to understand these "instructions" is the inner intentions I feel at the end of each day. Before I go to bed at night, I sit at the table and write down on a notepad what I feel I must do the next day in order to keep the pursuit of my dreams alive. I list things I want to accomplish or things that I feel need to be done in order to push my dreams forward.

By doing so, it frees my mind so I can fall asleep knowing that I've done everything possible this day to make my dreams come true; upholding my end of promise fulfillment.

We have such enthusiasm for the accomplishment of our dreams before we fall asleep, but then by the next morning we can barely remember who we are, let alone what we are all about. By looking at the previous night's list as we sip our tea or coffee, we are recapturing part of that previous days' enthusiasm and level of spiritual appreciation and motivation.

We Must Focus on God's Promises

Most of us don't feel worthy of asking God/Star to make a promise with us. We have self-esteem issues to work out. Asking God/Star to make a promise for this, or a promise for that, should be as easy and user-friendly to us as is breathing. Asking God/Star for a promise is like making wishes to a genie and hearing the genie answer, "Your wish is my command!" New Age philosophers would rather we say, "My wish is my command!" Jesus would have us say, "It is my will that the Father's will be done!"

The interesting thing I found out about promises is that just before a promise is made there is usually a petition stated; a proposal is made, a request for something to happen is stated out loud, and as one so asks, the promise is made. To promise means to pledge, to agree to, to give one's word. It also means to submit or present an idea, to make a motion, or to recommend. To make a proposal is like making a heartfelt, spirit-born petition; "Dear Father/Mother God, I petition you to agree to walk every step of the way with me just as I keep walking with you."

God would never expect us to do something God hasn't already done. God promises eternal life to all who would seek it. Seek and the way will be revealed. Knock and the door will be opened. Believe God is your Father, your Mother, for by all means you are Gods' child. Seek ye first the Kingdom of Heaven and all else will be added unto you.

Let those who have the ears to hear, listen. Become a 'Finder' first by becoming a 'Seeker' but don't stay a 'Seeker.' Just like a 'Leader' must first learn to be a 'Follower.'

Learn to keep God's commandments by putting God first in your considerations, and staying true to your mate, your family, and your community. Respect them and serve them with love.

A prayer is a good example of making a proposal for a promise. But how do we know what to ask for and what's best for us? Well, we can start by asking the "Infinite Is" to reveal to us what He designed us to ask for in the first place. Go ahead and ask the universal source of all that is, for an idea of what kinds of things are possible for you to go after, and then go after them.

You can't just be a bystander of life; you must also be a doer of life. We have a responsibility to ask God for promises and have the presence of mind to petition God for those proposals. We have a responsibility to ourselves, to not only "figure it out" for ourselves, but when we've done so to share it with others.

I am second eldest of ten children. At some point, when growing up, I knew I had to help the other kids and figure out how to make our family work best each day. I actually made a chart of all the chores that needed to be done and assigned to each child in rotation on a handmade calendar. I also created a multi-chambered box which I mounted on a wall in our kitchen to act as our Post Office to receive and send messages to each other, and distribute incoming mail.

No one told me to do these things. I now believe God had inspired me to do them because I genuinely wanted to help my parents handle so many kids. I thought, "Wouldn't it be great if someone were to do this, or do that?" Creativity was always one of my strong suits.

Living on this planet Earth, Urantia, is like living in a Petri dish, and if we don't wise-up, we are going to contaminate our living space beyond repair. So I propose we figure out how best to live with each other and promote the best in practices, principles, procedures, and prosperities for all, including our children's children.

The following excerpts from The Urantia Book serve as ideal observations concerning the ideas I'm putting forth regarding this treatise. They are specific references to places in The Urantia Book whereupon are found examples of how this information of The Great Urantian Agreement is to be put into context.

Said Jesus to his Apostles,
"You have entered upon this great work of teaching mortal man that he is a son of God. I have shown you the way; go forth to do your duty and be not weary in well doing. To you and to all who shall follow in your steps down through the ages, let me say: I always stand near, and my invitation-call is, and ever shall be, Come to me all you who labor and are heavy laden, and I will give you rest. Take my yoke upon you and learn of me, for I am true and loyal, and you shall find spiritual rest for your souls." The Urantia Book: 163:6.7

"And they found the Master's words to be true when they put his promises to the test. And since that day countless thousands also have tested and proved the surety of these same promises."
The Urantia Book: 163:6.8

"And all who heard these blessed words were greatly cheered. The Jewish teachings had been confused and uncertain regarding the survival of the righteous, and it was refreshing and inspiring for Jesus' followers to hear these very definite and positive words of assurance about the eternal survival of all true believers."
The Urantia Book: 146:3.8

I have come to understand how The Great Urantian Agreement relates to real life. These words of assurance are an example of God's promises to us; and when we not only believe these promises but also listen for instructions, we live full and meaningful lives. In our comings and goings we can listen for God's instructions on how, why, and when we can best apply love to serve our fellow man.

We can make our dreams come true!

Samples of God's Promises!

The following promises can be found in the Judeo/Christian Bible in various editions.

Old Testament

"Fear not...I am your shield, your exceedingly great reward." Genesis 15:1

"I will command my blessing upon you." Leviticus 25:21

"The Lord thy God, it is he who goes with you; he will not fail you, nor forsake you." Deuteronomy 31:6

"Acquaint now yourself with God and be at peace; thereby good shall come unto you." Job 22:21

"You shall also decree a thing to be, and it shall be established unto you: and the light shall shine upon your ways." Job 22:28

"Surely goodness and mercy shall follow me all the days of my life..." Psalm 23:6

"I will instruct you and teach you in the way which you shalt go: I will guide you with my eyes." Psalm 32:8

"Be still, and know that I am God." Psalm 46:10

"...no good thing will He withhold from them that walk along His paths." Psalm 84:11

"For He shall give His angels charge over you, to keep you in all your ways." Psalm 91:11

"The Lord is on my side; I fear not!" Psalm 118:6

"Behold, I will pour out my spirit unto you, I will make known my words to you." Proverbs 1:23

"In all thy ways acknowledge the presence of God, and he shall surely direct thy path." Proverbs 3:6

"I love them that love me; and those that seek me find me." Proverbs 8:17

"Now therefore listen to me, Oh my children: for happy and blessed are they that stay conscious of my presence. Hear my instruction, and be wise, and refuse it not." Proverbs 8:32-33

"If you are willing and obedient, you shall eat the good of the land." Isaiah 1:19

"No weapon that is formed against you shall prosper." Isaiah 54:17

"And you shall seek Me, and find Me, when you search for Me with all your heart." Jeremiah 29:13

"Call unto me, and I will answer you, and show you great and mighty things." Jeremiah 33:3

"The Lord thy God, within you is mighty; He will save, He will rejoice within you with joy and in song." Zephaniah 3:17

"Bring all the tithes into the store-house, that there is nourishment in mine house, and prove me now herewith, says the Lord of Hosts, if I will not open the windows of heaven and pour you out such a blessing, that there shall not be room enough to receive it all." Malachi 3:10

New Testament

"Seek you first the realm of God, and his righteousness; and all these things shall be added unto you." Matthew 6:33

"Ask and it shall be given you; seek, and you shall find; knock, and the door shall be opened unto you." Matthew 7:7

"Take no thought how or what you shall speak; for it shall be given you in the same hour what ye shall speak." Matthew 10:19

"...I will give you the keys to the kingdom of heaven." Matthew 16:19

"Lo, I am with you always, even unto the end of the world." Matthew 28:20

"If you can believe, all things are possible to him or her that trusts." Mark 9:23

Jesus said, "Put your trust in God." Mark 11:22

Jesus also said, "I give you my word, if you are ready to believe that you will receive whatever you ask for in prayer, it shall be done for you." Mark 11:24

"For with God nothing shall be impossible."
Luke 1:37

"Give and it shall be given unto you." Luke 6:38

"Fear not, little flock, for it is your Father's good pleasure to give you the kingdom."
Luke 12:32

"As many as received him, to them he gave power to become the sons and daughters of God."
John 1:12

"In my Father's house are many mansions: if it were not so, I would have told you. I go to prepare a place for you. And, if I go and prepare a place for you, I will come again and receive you unto myself; that where I am, there ye may be also." John 14:2-3

"I will not leave you comfortless: I will come to you." John 14:18

"If you abide in me, and my words abide in you, you shall ask what you will and it shall be done unto you." John 15:7

"...All things work together for good to those that love God." Romans 8:28

"For I am persuaded, that neither death, nor life, nor angels, nor principalities, nor powers, nor things present, nor things to come, nor height, nor depth, nor any other creature, shall be able to separate us from the love of God, which is exampled in Jesus." Romans 8:38-39

"But as it is written, eye hath not seen, nor ear heard, neither have entered into the heart of man, the things which God hath prepared for them that love him." 1 Corinthians 2:9

"He who soweth bountifully shall reap also bountifully." 2 Corinthians 9:6

"Let us hold fast the profession of our faith without wavering; for he is faithful that promised." Hebrews 10:23

"Faith is the substance of things hoped for, the evidence of things not yet seen." Hebrews 11:1

"Be not forgetful to entertain strangers: for thereby some have entertained angels unaware." Hebrews 13:2

"Blessed is the one that endures temptation: for when tried, they shall receive the crown of life, which the Lord has promised unto them that love." James 1:12

"Every good and perfect gift is from above, and comes down from the Father of Lights."
James 1:17

"The effectual fervent prayer of a sincere man avails much." James 5:16

"And this is the confidence that we have in him, that, if we ask anything according to his will, he hears us: and as we know that he hears us, whatsoever we ask, we know that we have the petitions that we desire of him." 1 John 5:14-15

Now, I submit some of my versions of God's promises.

I promise as you take care of each other, I will be there in your midst helping too.

I promise that as you have faith in something, that I have faith in you.

I promise that for every good deed you perform, thousands of good deeds will result, rippling across the universe, like the flapping wings of a butterfly.

I promise that as you come to know me within your heart I will not abandon you.

I promise you that love is the holiest of all spirits, and every breath you take is mine.

I promise to accompany you on your journey as you so let me.

I promise you that mankind is indeed a reflection of each other in spirit, and that whatsoever you do to the least of your brothers or sisters is being done unto me.

I promise that whatsoever you say shall be, shall be.

I promise as you learn to use my gift of free will constructively, and creatively, then truth, beauty, and goodness shall be yours now and forevermore.

I promise that heaven is a state of mind and spirit, not just a place; for everything and everywhere is a reflection of Paradise and you are welcome to be here.

I promise to be more than just God to you; but to be your Father, and Mother.

I promise to listen to all of your prayers.

I promise to take care of everything, you simply promise to believe in these promises and follow my instructions when I give them to you.

I promise you that hope will banish worry and fear, and that belief will harvest certainty in their place.

I promise to set the spiritually captive free, to bind up the brokenhearted and bring glad tidings and good news to the meek, to those who are humble enough to not be bothered by praise nor slander or by what others may think or speak of you or me.

I promise you will know what you need to know when you need to know it... just make sure you follow my instructions.

I promise to help you find, that which you've lost.

I promise to restore your belief in me and then bless you, beyond belief.

I promise, that when you pray for others and wish well to those around you, that others are also praying for your well-being too.

These and many more promises I make and keep with you ever more and as you so speak them.

All the above are examples of promises God made to "do everything."

*The aforementioned are suggested to be used only as a guideline.

God Will Take Care of Everything!

God works in mysterious ways. This part freaks many out. We would like to know in advance just "how" things will come about or how they will come to be. But that just doesn't happen in real life.

We must develop the sublime certainty of faith that God will do God's part, and manifest what will seem like a miracle for us, if and when one is needed or called for. During His public ministry, Jesus tried to not perform miracles, but sometimes the Father had a different idea.

As a bestowal Son, Jesus had the directive before coming to this world to rely on the will of His Father for the ultimate outcome of everything. "Not my will, but thy will be done," was foremost on His mind. Later in life, it eventually became, "Father, it is my will that your will be done."

When I was going on my first leave of absence in the early days of my military service in the U. S. Navy, I found myself giving a ride to a couple of Marines going to the airport, to go home on leave. I picked them up at the gate, and told them, as we left the base, that I could only take them so far to a drop off point in downtown Jacksonville on their way home via the local airport. Then, when we pulled up to a place off the highway where they would be getting out to continue their way to the airport, there were a number of young men standing on the sidewalk in front of a bar, smoking, laughing, and carrying on.

I had to stop the car because we were behind several cars, which had stopped at a red light. As we sat there in my convertible VW bug (with the top down), we were quickly surrounded by many of them asking for cigarettes and money. I knew this was a holdup and promptly started telling each of them "Jesus loves you!" At the back of my mind, I remembered the promise of Jesus that wherever two or more were gathered in his name, that He would be present. I felt I that I needed some divine assistance at that time, so I called on Him.

As I reached for my money to give to them, I noticed out of the corner of my eye, at the rear passenger side of the car, that a gun was pointed at me.

I told the gunman, "Jesus loves you too," and then came the roar of a gunshot with the feeling that I was hit from behind by a sledgehammer.

Slumping into the driver seat, my eyes came to focus on the most beautiful green traffic light I'd ever seen. I also heard in my mind the word, "Go!" The car had stalled so I turned the key and got us rolling down the road again. After turning the corner and driving about a hundred yards I pulled over and told one of the Marines to take over driving because I had just been shot. "What?" they yelled, "We thought that was just an M-80." "No," I replied, "I've been hit."

Driving a bit further we found a hospital and I was taken to a hospital bed where I lost track of the two Marines who had been my companions that evening. I never did get their full names. I wish I could reach out and thank them for being with me that night. Needless to say, while on a hospital bed from behind a curtain, I soon heard the voice of a woman saying, "Ronnie, one of your students is over here."

I soon met the faces of people who were going to be my adopted family for the holidays as I wasn't going home that year. Earlier, during the evening at a local restaurant, one of their daughters had become violently ill and they brought her to the same hospital. Then, when they found me, the child was instantly better. I knew God was watching out for me by that time and I basked, unknown, in the Joy of God doing "everything."

The doctors and police investigators decided to leave the bullet in me because they were certain they didn't need the ballistics off the bullet. They said they had found the 38 caliber "snub nose" revolver that was used on me at a different crime scene later that night where another 18 year old had been shot through the neck and was killed.

I guess Jesus held my body at a certain angle so that the bullet would only go in so far and then stop, thereby not killing me. Yay! Thank you Jesus!

I still have the bullet in me, by the way.

Things happen in life that we just can't explain.

I didn't want to be alone that Christmas, and so God had worked it out that I could be with a loving family.

If we just knew The Great Agreement was in effect, we could then enjoy the benefits of applying it more often. If we knew we were having our wishes answered, then we would be wishing more often.

Yes! God works in mysterious ways, so hang onto your hat, the ride is about to get pretty grand.

Bliss

You don't have to feel good to start, but you do have to start to feel good.

To instill bliss in myself, I imagine each of the cells in my body are like little puppy dogs with their tails wagging like crazy. I can feel the cells in my body vibrating and enjoy the feeling as it permeates the room I'm in; blooming like a flowering tree.

Theorist Joseph Campbell eloquently spoke of the hero's journey as a reality road taken by heroes and heroines whom follow their bliss. Wow! So how do I best follow my bliss? And what does feeling good have to do with the Great Urantian Agreement? If your heart is in your dreams, this is how you feel when you make a wish and have those wishes fulfilled.

Bliss is the joy of life that empowers your body, mind, and soul. It can best be perceived as feeling happy while being conscious; conscious of the presence of a happy mind and body, imitating the "divine" personality within. If you can't "feel" good, then the cells of your body aren't vibrating to their highest potential and you are not enjoying the "fruits of the spirit" that Jesus inspires us to produce.

It's at this point that I wish to insert the following excerpt from The Urantia Book where Jesus is speaking to his apostles after the last supper and wished to instruct them about staying in touch with him even though he is preparing to leave them.

The Vine and the Branches

Then Jesus stood up again and continued teaching his apostles: "I am the true vine, and my Father is the husbandman. I am the vine, and you are the branches. And the Father requires of me only that you shall bear much fruit. The vine is pruned only to increase the fruitfulness of its branches. Every branch coming out of me which bears no fruit, the Father will take away. Every branch which bears fruit, the Father will cleanse that it may bear more fruit. Already are you clean through the word I have spoken, but you must continue to be clean. You must abide in me, and I in you; the branch will die if it is separated from the vine. As the branch cannot bear fruit except it abides in the vine, so neither can you yield the fruits of loving service except you abide in me. Remember: I am the real vine, and you are the living branches. He who lives in me, and I in him, will bear much fruit of the spirit and experience the supreme joy of yielding this spiritual harvest. If you will maintain this living spiritual connection with me, you will bear abundant fruit. If you abide in me and my words live in you, you will be able to commune freely with me, and then can my living spirit so infuse you that you may ask whatsoever my spirit wills and do all this with the assurance that the Father will grant us our petition. Herein is the Father glorified: that the vine has many living branches, and that every branch bears much fruit. And when the world sees these fruit-bearing branches—my friends who love one another, even as I have loved them—all men will know that you are truly my disciples.

"As the Father has loved me, so have I loved you. Live in my love even as I live in the Father's love. If you do as I have taught you, you shall abide in my love even as I have kept the Father's word and evermore abide in his love."

The Jews had long taught that the Messiah would be "a stem arising out of the vine" of David's ancestors, and in commemoration of this olden teaching a large emblem of the grape and its attached vine decorated the entrance to Herod's temple. The apostles all recalled these things while the Master talked to them this night in the upper chamber.

But great sorrow later attended the misinterpretation of the Master's inferences regarding prayer. There would have been little difficulty about these teachings if his exact words had been remembered and subsequently truthfully recorded. But as the record was made, believers eventually regarded prayer in Jesus' name as a sort of supreme magic, thinking that they would receive from the Father anything they asked for. For centuries honest souls have continued to wreck their faith against this stumbling block. How long will it take the world of believers to understand that prayer is not a process of getting your way but rather a program of taking God's way, an experience of learning how to recognize and execute the Father's will? It is entirely true that, when your will has been truly aligned with his, you can ask anything conceived by that will-union, and it will be granted. And such a will-union is effected by and through Jesus even as the life of the vine flows into and through the living branches.

When there exists this living connection between divinity and humanity, if humanity should thoughtlessly and ignorantly pray for selfish ease and vainglorious accomplishments, there could be only one divine answer: more and increased bearing of the fruits of the spirit on the stems of the living branches. When the branch of the vine is alive, there can be only one answer to all its petitions: increased grape bearing. In fact, the branch exists only for, and can do nothing except, fruit bearing, yielding grapes. So does the true believer exist only for the purpose of bearing the fruits of the spirit: to love man as he himself has been loved by God— that we should love one another, even as Jesus has loved us.

And when the Father's hand of discipline is laid upon the vine, it is done in love, in order that the branches may bear much fruit. And a wise husbandman cuts away only the dead and fruitless branches.

Jesus had great difficulty in leading even his apostles to recognize that prayer is a function of spirit-born believers in the spirit-dominated kingdom. The Urantia Book 180:2

We have a fragment of the personality of our Divine Father / Mother within us. This fragment knows how to be happy; knows what to be proud of, and how to desire truth, beauty, and goodness. We can turn our focus upon this divine being within and learn to listen to its voice and inspiration. We can use this God given feature toward our benefit and the benefit of those around us. Let's listen for the will of God.

Spend your days meditating on the joys of time filled with a lively sense of gratitude and appreciation for so much prosperity and fruitfulness. Be in gratitude for the many blessings and meaningful succession of days filled with the presence of those whom we love and are loved by.

When you are grateful, you are instilling positive energy into the unified field of the Universe through being joyful and enthusiastic for your success and the success of others. These previously unknown energies are a spiritual reality which, begin to grow and expand by being shared with others. It is an eternal quality that will endure forever.

Often harsh, the only fair way to gauge anyone or anything is by results. What kind of results are you getting in life? If you don't like something, then change it.

Can you do the following? Reach deep inside your mind and find something that makes you feel physical joy: a sense of bliss. Found it?

OK, now picture that every cell in your body is like tiny, happy little puppies wagging their tails. Then let this feeling snowball until the feeling fills the room you're in. Then let the feeling grow to encompass your house... the block you live on... your neighborhood, and then your city. Blow it out further still to wrap the entire world, and then the Solar System. Become familiar with what you feel like when you are extremely happy and filled with joy. Be a Star. You are the light of the world.

And, if you don't like little puppies for some reason, picture something else that helps you actually feel happiness.

What is the point of it all, you may ask? Well, your destiny is to "thrive" as a Son or Daughter of God, to "Go forth and multiply!" To feel happy, grand, and be abundant! To be a Star!

By the way, this life is but the mudroom to the bigger mansion of eternal existence we enter into after we die, so please pay attention.

When you wish upon a Star,
your dreams come true.

Afterword

God will make sure the engines of life stay turned on. God will make sure the sun continues to shine and be the center of our solar system, and God will continue to be the source of, and host of our world's entire resources.

Everything your eyes light upon was once only a thought in someone's head. That's right! Things we take for granted once did not exist.

Like the telephone, the television, the internet and so on, things in nature were once just a twinkle in the eye of God; just a thought in God's mind. And then God spoke the word and the word became physical, became flesh.

As we mature and develop faculties of mental management regarding things in our lives, we learn to take creative thought and apply it to the mind, therefore impressing that thought on the formless substance of the Universe and make it come into being.

The future is yet to happen. It is awaiting our arrival to participate in creating the present in the presence of the Creator. It is fulfilling the directive of "Be Ye Perfect!"

God will take care of every breath we take and every beat of our heart. God will be with us as we stay busy perfecting our world. God will take care of everything.

Now, isn't that nice to know?

www.ingramcontent.com/pod-product-compliance
Lightning Source LLC
Chambersburg PA
CBHW072051290426
44110CB00014B/1637